What People Are Saying About

WHAT MATTERS?
For family wellbeing

A great book, and easy to read for busy parents.
Wook Hamilton, Head of Development at the Parent-Infant Foundation, UK

Clear but gentle and reassuring — this book will help with the best but toughest job in the world — being a 'good enough' parent.
Dr Sally Smith, CEO, 'peeple' Oxford

In this elegantly written and helpful book, Rosemary Roberts smuggles in a lifetime's experience and scholarship of early childhood learning and development while making it both accessible and reassuring. She helps carers think about how to be good companions to babies and young children, without neglecting themselves. This book is indispensable for anyone spending time with babies and young children.
Chris Mowles, Professor of Complexity and Management, University of Hertfordshire

This book fills a significant gap in literature for parents, especially first-time parents. I love the writing and book structure — both are pitch perfect. Plain English without jargon is hard to do for those with academic qualifications.
Dr Anne Meade, Independent Education Consultant, New Zealand

T0182528

WHAT MATTERS?
For family wellbeing

Babies, young children, and
their companions' mental health
and happiness

WHAT MATTERS?
For family wellbeing

Babies, young children, and
their companions' mental health
and happiness

Rosemary Roberts

BOOKS

London, UK
Washington, DC, USA

CollectiveInk

First published by O-Books, 2024
O-Books is an imprint of Collective Ink Ltd.,
Unit 11, Shepperton House, 89 Shepperton Road, London, N1 3DF
office@collectiveinkbooks.com
www.collectiveinkbooks.com
www.o-books.com

For distributor details and how to order please visit the 'Ordering' section on our website.

Text copyright: Rosemary Roberts 2023

ISBN: 978 1 80341 622 9
978 1 80341 628 1 (ebook)
Library of Congress Control Number: 2023942285

A CIP catalogue record for this book is available from the British Library.

Design: Lapiz Digital Services

UK: Printed and bound by CPI Group (UK) Ltd, Croydon, CR0 4YY
Printed in North America by CPI GPS partners

The author of this book does not dispense medical advice or prescribe the use of any technique as a form of treatment for physical, emotional, or medical problems without the advice of a physician, either directly or indirectly. The intent of the author is only to offer information of a general nature to help you in your quest for emotional and spiritual well-being. In the event you use any of the information in this book for yourself, which is your constitutional right, the author and the publisher assume no responsibility for your actions.

We operate a distinctive and ethical publishing philosophy in all areas of our business, from our global network of authors to production and worldwide distribution.

Contents

About the Author

Dr Rosemary Roberts is an early years consultant and writer. She holds a post-graduate diploma from the Tavistock Clinic UK in Psychoanalytic Observational Studies, and a PhD 'Companionable learning: the development of resilient wellbeing from birth to three' (2007). In 1999 she was awarded an OBE for services to children. She has worked in nursery, primary and higher education and the voluntary sector, in the UK and latterly in Australia. She has published two books: *Self Esteem and Early Learning* (Sage Publications, 3rd ed., 2006) and *Wellbeing from Birth* (Sage Publications, 2010). She has three children and four grandchildren, and is a Quaker especially concerned for mental health and social justice. 'What Matters?' is drawn from all these elements of her life so far.

My warm thanks to critical readers Kate, Jayne, Anne, Katie, Alison, Vanessa, Hannah, Joy, Christine, Kathy, Louise, Julia, Nicola, Ben, and Olivia, who read early drafts and suggested many helpful amendments; and to my family and friends for their patience and encouragement.

Chapter 1

Getting Started

1. Is 'What Matters' for you?
2. When is the best time to read 'What Matters'?
3. What do parents usually hope for their children?
4. In this changing world, what matters now?
5. What are the main messages of 'What Matters'?

1. Is 'What Matters' for you?

These days babies and young children may have a lot of people in their lives. The needs of babies themselves haven't changed much, but the world in which they live is suddenly very different. Babies may well have many 'companions': people who they see often and know well, who are loving or affectionate with them. Many people have had a positive and secure early childhood themselves, but not everyone. Whatever your own childhood roots are, companionship with a new baby can bring much joy, sometimes unexpectedly.

If you are a mother, father, partner, or primary carer, of course you matter most. Other important players in young children's lives might be grandparents, siblings, aunts, uncles and cousins; members of the family. As well, there might be family friends, neighbours, childcarers, or companionable key people in day-care. It can be quite a cast of companions! If you are reading this perhaps you are, or will be, a 'companion' and you want to make the most of it. If so, this book is for you.

What Matters is for very busy and often completely exhausted readers. It is deliberately short and without references (but see 'About the Author' for validity). Post-pandemic, our lives are comparatively separated, because of masks, social distancing and the like. What Matters is a timely reminder about the importance of relationships in early childhood, nurturing babies and young children's mental health and resilience. This is not about being perfect parents and carers, but finding out about *good enough*, a consistent theme throughout the book.

2. When is the best time to read 'What Matters'?

During the first three years is good (and the first year is probably best) because very early experiences lay the most important long-lasting foundations for physical, social, emotional and learning development. If you are parents looking forward to a new baby, about halfway through the pregnancy can be a good time, when plans are starting to take shape and the confidence that this book can give you might help. But it is never too late, because What Matters is based on findings that can be useful throughout life.

3. What do parents usually hope for their children?

When parents are asked about their hopes for their children, the first reply is usually 'to be healthy and happy'. This generally seems to be the starting point, although of course other wellbeing elements matter too. There are plenty of 'how to' books and online advice available on what to do in particular situations, but they are often contradictory. What Matters is about families finding a consistent general approach to everyone's wellbeing: how to be feeling all right in yourself, and with other people, and reasonably coping. It is about ways to bring up healthy, happy babies and young children, with *good enough* wellbeing and resilience.

4. In this changing world, what matters now?

The world has changed astonishingly fast, especially since the turn of the century. These changes are making an enormous impact on the childhoods of the youngest children. For babies and young children especially, it is worth briefly mentioning just three areas: first, the latest neuroscience research; second, the impact of the COVID-19 pandemic; and third, expanding childcare needs.

1. Latest Research

Since the 1990s, the neuroscience of early childhood has provided us with much solid and consistent information about when and how our brains develop. We know that early experiences don't stay in early childhood but continue to make a difference to life outcomes. We are told that about 90% of the neural networks that lay down future health, wellbeing and life-long learning are thought to develop during a child's earliest years, from birth (indeed in utero) to five years. The message for parents and carers is reassuringly straightforward. In summary, what babies need for strong and healthy neural networks is caring, responsive adults.

2. The Impact of the COVID-19 Pandemic on Families

Much more well-designed research is needed about this, especially in relation to the youngest children. So far, UK studies report school closures, disrupted access to healthcare, an increase in domestic violence and worsening mental health in families. Teachers report children struggling with emotional wellbeing as well as ability to learn language and numeracy skills when starting school. Globally, there are reports of a rise in violence generally, worsening mental health, and a surge in poverty. Families in lower income countries have been hit the hardest. Save The Children says: 'COVID-19 is the biggest global health, education and economic crisis of our lifetime and has impacted every child around the world'. What Matters is in part a response to this appalling picture, offering a positive and financially manageable way forward for families with the youngest children.

3. Expanding Childcare Needs, and Diminishing Options

With more parents working, the need for good childcare has increased over recent years. There are many wonderful daycare settings to be found, perhaps not always in expensive buildings with shiny toys, but where babies and young children's lives are happily full of consistent emotional warmth with caring, responsive adults.

But the cost of childcare is now prohibitive for many families. Some nurseries are closing, while remaining staff are doing a valiant job with little training, shockingly low pay and little public acknowledgment or appreciation of their crucially important work. There is a crisis in the sector, while at the same time more parents need to find childcare that works both for themselves and for their children.

In public debates about childcare provision the focus is on the ruinously high cost to parents, and on national economics and workforce requirements. Solutions are seen in terms of increased access to daycare settings. The needs of the youngest children themselves are very rarely mentioned. In policy terms, this failure to prioritise them and explore ways to nurture them as the most precious resource for the future that we have makes absolutely no sense. What matters for them is consistent, caring, responsive adult companions. So in this challenging childcare context, exploring the possibility of 'companiable' care at home, or if affordable with a companionable childcarer, are surely important options for some families. Solid government policies to support those families would make absolute sense.

5. What are the main messages of 'What Matters'?

What Matters is all about companionable ways of being with children. As it happens these ways do not involve spending money, a fortunate factor in a world where so many families are struggling financially. Almost all babies have at least several 'companions', people they see often, know well and who are loving or affectionate with them. Babies with one or two companions in their lives will be fine, while for many it is the more the merrier. These companionable relationships with genuinely caring, responsive adults are at the heart of the eight What Matters chapters: Getting Started; Companions Matter; Belonging-and-Behaviour Matters; Caring Matters; Learning Matters; Doing Matters; You Matter; and Looking Ahead. They are about laying *good enough* foundations for lifelong mental health and wellbeing.

But what about physical health? We know this matters very much, right from the start. However, in relation to health and illness there are already many reliable people to consult and well-researched places to find out what to do; in health services, online, in libraries and in bookshops. Many parents will already be well-informed about their child's physical needs and development. Most have the benefit of long-established services such as midwives, health visitors and doctor practices to turn to when in doubt.

So the main messages are about managing a *good enough* balance. But we all, children and adults, go through periods of imbalance. For instance a severe illness, financial worries, feeling excluded over a long period, the exhaustion of the months following pregnancy and childbirth, or a collapse in confidence can put us out of balance. Thinking about the different chapters here can help us to identify what is missing, for our children or for ourselves. They may help us to hang on through hard times, perhaps taking appropriate action if possible, and looking forward to better days.

There is much that parents and carers already know or can easily find out and What Matters is not about looking up what to do in a crisis. Instead, it offers a way to consider a generally consistent approach, giving you the confidence to find your way through the sometimes contradictory advice about what to do for the best. What Matters is for thinking about what matters to *you* as companions, for your babies and young children's health and happiness and your own — not just now, but throughout life.

Chapter 2

Companions Matter

1. What does being a companion mean?
2. What's special about companions?
3. What is our first language?
4. Do babies feel stress?
5. How can we be *good enough* companions?

1. What does being a companion mean?

Being a 'companion' with a baby or small child comes up in this book again and again. Connecting companionably with the youngest children is a way of paying attention. It feeds every baby's need to feel safe and loved. What Matters is about many different ways that this can happen, and the word 'together' is a frequent reminder of babies need for connection. It is a kind of caring attachment, which is one of the greatest gifts we can give. These companionable friendships are wonderful both for babies and young children, and for parents and carers themselves. It's worth making the most of existing companions and, as time goes by, if possible looking around for new ones.

2. What's special about companions?

All babies and young children delight in attention from their companions — the people they know and love best. To be watching and listening companionably to a baby or young child is a kind of 'mindfulness', a way of paying attention that feeds babies' need to know they are securely safe and loved. It is usually their companions body language that lets the youngest children know when they have our companionable attention, especially when we are simply watching and listening to them, looking interested but not necessarily saying anything. That may be all they need, particularly if they are feeling anxious and trying to tell us something in their own way. If they are trying to manage something difficult like going to sleep, not dropping a toy, or finishing their tea, sometimes their need is simply for undivided attention.

But sometimes we are busy and children cannot get our attention in spite of their best efforts. Children seeking our attention are asking for it because, from their point of view, they genuinely need it. Surprisingly, this is often disapprovingly called 'attention seeking', when actually it is, usually, skilfully judged communication. A toddler who is getting nowhere by just looking hopeful might try hugging adult knees. If that fails, maybe a little poking, or dropping something on your toes will work. No good? Then maybe making a mess by tipping things onto the floor or making the baby cry, or even picking up a sharp knife, or drawing on the walls. Of course then there's trouble.

It's usually not that they actually want to do these things, it's because they really need us. Irritated or even angry attention from a companion usually feels better to them than being ignored. This can be a real dilemma when you are already exhausted and trying frantically to keep on top of everything. Distractions such as TV, a biscuit or a dummy may bring temporary peace and save our sanity. But what such apparently 'bad' behaviour may really be about is a real need for companionable attention. In that case the need remains, and maybe even grows.

If this sounds familiar, the good news is that it needn't be like this. Once small children have learned that we will, somehow, give them our attention when they need it, they don't seem to need it nearly so much. It is a kind of pay back for giving children companionable attention as much as we can. And it isn't just children needing to feel safe and loved.

Because companionship works both ways, it is also about how they learn to 'pay attention' to the world around them and that includes us.

3. What is our first language?

We think of a child's first language as the words they use when they start to talk, going from babbling through to learning how to express their feelings and asking for the things they want. Now that we have increasingly more different languages and cultures all around us, does this cause problems for them with making new friends or settling down easily in daycare or school? Maybe your child's first language is Mandarin, Hindi, Spanish or English, but is it really the first? In reality, words are our second language, while every baby's very first language is a gloriously universal one: body language. Glorious because we all share it, and also because babies are born fluent! They are very attentive watchers of their companion's body language and if we, their companions, are able to be as attentive as they are, everyone is off to a flying start.

From the day they are born, babies are able to have wonderful conversations with people, conversations that become more fascinating and satisfying as time goes by, without ever speaking a word. Watching the way babies respond to smiles, gentle greetings and questions shows that these are indeed conversations, taking turns to and fro. Babies are astonishingly good at starting conversations too. They do it by catching our eyes, with smiles, and delighted wriggles when they see the person they want to talk with. And that person says things with body language too: the loving look that says, "I'm happy to see you", the gentle touch that says, "you're precious to me", or maybe the worried frown that says, "Now, what's the matter?"

These body language exchanges are the main ways that babies and young children first communicate with us, their companions. And it's often our tone of voice, rather than what we actually say that makes sense to a small child. For example, "Come here you rascal" might mean "I'm cross with you" or it might mean "I want to give you a hug, I love you so much". Perhaps this lasts all our lives. Does what we actually say or hear ever mean more than the body language and tone of voice that goes with the words?

We can use all of our senses to connect with the world — to everyone and everything in it — and this is especially true for the youngest children. Touch, smell and taste are just as important as seeing and hearing. As adults we mostly rely on seeing and hearing, but in our early years, as we develop from babies into young children, touch, smell and taste are great ways of 'finding out' too. No wonder everything goes into babies' mouths!

4. Do babies feel stress?
There seems to be a prevailing myth that the lives of babies and young children are carefree and that stress comes with adulthood. We call ourselves stressed when we are anxious, exhausted, fearful, frustrated, insecure, overwhelmed or misunderstood. Why we think that these conditions do not apply to babies and young children sometimes, is hard to understand.

Here are some of the realities. A baby who is left in the care of someone before really knowing them may feel anxious, fearful and insecure. At the end of a long day most babies are exhausted, and sometimes feel overwhelmed. No matter how hard we try to get it right, it is entirely normal that we often misunderstand what a baby needs. And the frustrations of helplessness are of course considerable. All these are normal conditions of babies and young children's lives. They experience the ebb and flow of normal daily stress, just as we do.

Normal levels of the hormone cortisol are what our bodies need. But cortisol floods the brain in times of stress. Since the discovery that levels of cortisol can be measured quite simply in saliva, much more is known about the impact of stress and consequent high cortisol levels on babies' overall development. Why does too much cortisol matter? It increases blood pressure and blood sugar levels both in children and adults and it suppresses the immune system. What helps to reduce damaging cortisol levels in babies is promptly responsive parents and carers and gentle affectionate touch and cuddles.

For babies, stress is almost always about physical survival — they cannot survive on their own, and they need milk, warmth and security. A frightening sense of helplessness may wash over them when someone does not respond promptly to their distress. Almost always, a stressed baby needs companionable attention as soon as possible to feel better. And when we give companionable attention we are most likely to succeed in figuring out what else a baby needs. Sometimes it may be just simply our attention that is needed, but it may be that the baby is tired and hungry; or needing a nappy change; frightened or in pain; or bored, lonely and wanting company. It is when we pay careful, companionable attention that we are most likely to get the 'diagnosis' right.

Crying babies are never being naughty. They are signalling that something is wrong. But parents and other companions can't know from the start what a baby needs. It can be a scary process of trial and error, especially to begin with. Paying companionable attention is the easiest and fastest way to start knowing what to do, building confidence all round.

5. How can we be *good enough* companions?
The chapters in this book have many overlapping connections. They are about what matters: belonging and behaviour, caring, learning, and things to do together. And they are about the wellbeing of companions too. These overlapping ideas can make

things easier for everyone, but no-one can possibly do them all the time. Being a companion is not so much about *what* we do, but *how* we do things together. Being *good enough* companions is about living day-to-day ordinary life, companionably together: nothing special.

Chapter 3

Belonging-and-Behaviour Matters

1. Why does belonging matter?
2. How does a baby's identity take shape?
3. How do babies and young children learn about belonging?
4. What has belonging got to do with behaviour?
5. What about 'spoiling' children?
6. Can routines help?
7. How can companions prevent so many tantrums?
8. What matters most about behaviour?

1. Why does belonging matter?

Belonging matters, for happiness. Perhaps 'feeling contented' is a better way to put it, since belonging and contentment go hand in hand. Instead of making lists of things to do with a baby or young child that will be 'good' for them, or simply to get through the day, another way is to watch out for your favourite activities together. What are the things you both find satisfying, sharing each other's complete attention on whatever you are doing together? Maybe cuddles, playing, or looking at a favourite book? Just being ourselves in everyday life is so much easier than suddenly trying to be different. There is so much pressure, both within us and out in the world, to compete with the unrealistic and sometimes fake versions of parenthood often displayed on social media, but it doesn't matter what other parents are doing (or say they are doing). What works for you and the baby is all that matters. The feeling that we belong together and the conversations that we share will build our child's wellbeing and our own.

Babies' belonging is about feeling safe and feeling loved and accepted.

The process of building belonging and security, both for babies and parents, can start earlier than many people realise. During pregnancy, from 22 weeks a baby's hearing begins to develop rapidly, so by that stage your baby will frequently be hearing your voice, favourite music and even lullabies and songs you might sing. Familiar voices and the sounds and music that your baby has come to know in the womb, may be especially comforting after being born.

2. How does a baby's identity take shape?

Incredibly early on, babies and young children start to develop a sense of what sort of person they are. Perhaps they feel lovable, acceptable, enjoyable company even. How does this happen? It's a kind of mirroring process. When companions love them they will feel loveable. When companions accept them they will feel acceptable. When companions obviously enjoy being with them, they learn to see themselves as good company. In every *companionable* moment they are learning to feel good about themselves. When this happens in the earliest years, an important and permanent foundation is being laid for life-long wellbeing.

Babies and young children are like sponges, soaking up everything that happens to them and around them. They do this whether we want them to or not, taking in the good with the not-so-good. Sadly, a lot of the not-so-good can lead them to feel (unconsciously of course) unlovable and unacceptable, negative feelings that later may be hard to shift. But most are likely to end up with a normally mixed sense of self. And as this book is about being *good enough*, some not-so-good experiences in the mix are not a disaster. This is normality. Since no-one can be perfect, aiming for perfection is setting ourselves up for failure. But it is useful for companions to know about the mirroring process, and how building *good enough* positive self-concept takes shape.

For all of us, there are questions about two sorts of self-concept, one sort leading to the other. First, as described above, is about what kind of person we feel we are. How do we see ourselves? And the second question, following on from the first, is about fitting in. Where and with whom do we belong?

3. How do babies and young children learn about belonging?

Children need a sense of their own identity in order to get a feeling for where they belong. This occurs at first with their parents, then maybe their wider family and friends, and later with their friends at their nursery or school and in their community. This is about their sense of identity *in relation to other people.* How do they 'fit' with the people around them? What feels right? Who will they identify with? In the normal course of events the youngest children may sometimes spend time playing outside the close family circle. They might play with extended family and friends, with other families, with groups of friends in parks and playgrounds. This is how they begin to get a sense of what it feels like to belong, and perhaps what *not* belonging feels like too. The child who grows up with a normally mixed sense of self and with a developing sense of what belonging and not belonging feel like, together with feeling loveable and acceptable, will be off to a flying start in adolescence.

Children develop a sense of belonging to places, too. This starts with places like their own cot, their pushchair, the kitchen, the road outside, even the local park or playground. Having to leave these familiar places and go where both people and places are new may sometimes be difficult for them. Companions who can remain part of their care during these times of transition will provide important security.

4. What has belonging got to do with behaviour?

Behaviour goes hand in hand with belonging. It's like two sides of one coin. We might belong in a special friendship or with a partner, and those relationships come with boundaries and expectations about what kind of behaviour is acceptable, even if we don't talk about them. Then there is the family, where there will certainly be expectations about behaviour both for children and adults, although they may not be explained aloud. Daycare settings and schools come with rules about everyone's behaviour and when you are accepted into that sort of community you are expected to behave in certain ways. Echoing a primary maths lesson on equations, we could say that belonging plus expectations equals behaviour. In order to be accepted and to carry on belonging we need to be aware of how to behave and how *not* to behave. Belonging with someone, or belonging somewhere, means that our behaviour matters. Talking about this clearly and companionably in early childhood is enormously helpful for young children, for teenagers, and for family wellbeing generally.

5. What about 'spoiling' children?

Some say that babies and young children living with companionable loving and acceptance all the time leads to 'spoiling' them. But for babies, because of what we know about child development, this fear of spoiling them isn't an issue. Crying is a baby's way of telling us that they need us. They are too young to be trying to manipulate us, hardly yet even being aware that they are a separate person. Meeting a baby's needs as well as possible in the early months is a tough and utterly exhausting but essential job for the all-important 'attached' companion, usually the mother. It is what it is. So there's no such thing as 'spoiling' a new baby. These early months are when we are learning about their needs, and how to meet them.

Later, as the companionable dialogue develops, there will be times for 'yes' and times for 'no'. And later still, sometimes when the answer has been 'no', small children begin to discover how they can make their parents say **"Oh all right!"**. So the companionable answer in relation to toddlers and older children is this. That when children are a little older, **on one important condition**, there's no such thing as too much attention and comforting, no such thing as too much playing, talking and laughing together, no such thing as too many hugs, presents or treats. But that one condition matters. It is that parents and other companions give these things **because they genuinely want to**, not because the child has 'made' them. Being *companionably* in control is about mostly saying 'yes' to things, together with the occasional, essential, gently firm 'no'.

'Spoiling' children does matter. It matters when they will not take 'no' for an answer, always wanting their own way. For a few children this can't be helped or perhaps has happened already, but it still needs managing. It's never too late to start being companionable, paying attention and being positive, but staying in control. And it matters when, as older children and adults, they are insensitive to other people's feelings, still always wanting their own way. But it's safe to go for loving and accepting and making the most of every companionable moment, so long as these things are freely given, and expectations about behaviour are part of the picture too.

Young children need their companions to be reasonably predictable, as far as possible, in what they say and do. How well a baby comes to know what to expect from parents and other companions depends mostly on how consistent those companions can manage to be with the child. Of course companions, even two parents, will do some things differently from each other. But as long as each person is fairly predictable, children soon learn what to expect from each different companion. It is sudden changes in an adult's mood and behaviour that is puzzling and unsettling for them. Learning to know what to expect from each of us is what helps a small child feel safe.

A useful saying for life with young children, and maybe for adults too, is: 'Say yes as often as you can (the loving, accepting bit); and when you say no, mean it' (the discipline bit). Parenting advice is so often to say 'no'; saying 'yes' as much as possible is *less* mentioned. But instead of saying no more or less automatically, it may be worth getting into the habit of *first* thinking "Can I say yes?"

Saying 'yes' often really is the key to saying 'no' successfully. Rigidly over-using 'no' leads to a downward spiral of frustration and insecurity, though on the fewer occasions when you *have* to say 'no' because it *really* matters, it's important to stick to it. Meanwhile saying 'yes' as often as possible leads to an upward spiral of satisfaction and security. So the bottom line is 'Say yes as often as you can; and when you say no, mean it'.

6. Can routines help?

Routines can support families a great deal and companionable routines also help children to feel safe and secure. Small children usually want to be like the people they love most, so getting the hang of family routines comes easily when everyone does them together. And small children are a great deal happier, more settled and less often frustrated when they are 'in the know' about what is going to happen next.

This way of learning about what will happen next can be helpful in several ways. It works when there is a bit of a routine to the day especially around the main events, such as getting up, going out, mealtimes, bedtimes and so on. Babies and young children learn incredibly quickly from their experiences. When good things, happening together with you (like getting dressed, having breakfast and going out) begin to happen in the same order as yesterday and the day before, they feel safer and more settled. People often think that the benefits of routines are about control and discipline, but *companionable* routines really are one of the easiest and quickest paths to a settled, contented baby or small child, and contented companions too. And if tomorrow's routine has to be different from today's, it helps to talk about it before tomorrow arrives. That way, the small child is still 'in the know'.

Companionable routines are when someone, or even perhaps everyone in a family, joins in with things together, such as ways to behave at mealtimes, getting dressed or going to bed. These routines are a consequence of belonging in that family. It is as though the companion with the child is saying "This is what we do here, let's do it together". This is what the two sides of the coin Belonging-and-Behaviour look like in action.

These things can take a while to settle down though and sometimes people give up too soon. When someone says they have tried everything, it may be that they didn't try one thing for long enough before trying another. But with success comes confidence and a growing sense of freedom and independence for everyone in the family. Children begin to get the idea of knowing what to expect, and to feel good about themselves.

Routines become outdated over time, but they can work for longer when companions are responsive and flexible, keeping in touch with children's ever-changing needs and remembering to say yes as often as they can. The same routines can still operate well as a basic security structure within which all sorts of variations can happen. If, for example, you normally get dressed before eating breakfast, maybe one day the breakfast is ready before the child is dressed, or the baby was really hungry today as soon as they woke up. The option occasionally to do things differently if you, the adult companion, decide to do so, is always there. And if you find yourself thinking that one of your family routines has turned into a rod for your own back, then perhaps it's time to get together and think again.

7. How can companions prevent so many tantrums?

Routines can help to reduce tantrums, because knowing what will happen next tends to give children a bit of a sense of control. Unexpected happenings are very hard for the youngest children, especially when they fall right outside the usual patterns of the day. Even things that you think will delight them, like a day out with a picnic, or a longer-than-usual play session with another family, can be difficult. And when small children are really enjoying something and the time comes to clear up, switch off or go home, there can be tantrums because of suddenly having to stop. Even when they were not even enjoying something particularly, having to stop *suddenly and unexpectedly* can trigger a tantrum.

This is when it helps a lot to prepare them about what is going to happen next, perhaps with the 'five minutes to go' alert. Of course they won't know exactly how long you mean by five minutes, but to say "I'm going to turn that off in five minutes because we're going out to meet Grandpa" or "You've got five minutes more playing and then we need to go home and make tea" can be a great help. Then the child gets a little warning before being whisked away, and also knows what is coming next. This makes life much easier all round and usually keeps things calmer than they might have been.

"I *wish* I knew what they want!" is probably a familiar thought, especially for new parents. When tears and tantrums seem to be happening all the time, days can feel exhaustingly long and challenging. Usually, tantrums are about frustration. Small children (like teenagers later) have to live with a high degree of dependence together with a passionate desire to be independent. Perhaps it's not surprising that for small children the combination of extreme frustration together with limited ability to explain what they want results in tantrums. But as children get better at explaining and adults get better at listening companionably, tantrums become less frequent.

Some people suggest that ignoring a tantrum is best. But is it companionable? Rather than going away just when a toddler feels so angry and out of control that it's frightening for them, the companionable way is to stay nearby, making sure they are safe, paying attention but not talking until the storm has passed. Then perhaps a drink and a cuddle and maybe later a talk about it. Looking back together after a while at what happened and beginning to learn how to describe their emotions helps children to feel less overwhelmed and frightened, and ultimately more in control of themselves in difficult situations. Talking together with someone companionable helps with understanding and accepting difficult emotions — an important ability in adolescence and adulthood too.

8. What matters most about behaviour?

Research has shown that rigidly authoritarian parenting, that takes little account of children's feelings and needs, is bad for children and often does not end well. Equally, very permissive parenting in which anything goes, tends not to end well either. Children need companions who are clear and consistent about what is expected. In an ideal world, companions who are in charge explain gently but firmly what they expect, keeping on top of things by reminding in advance, and warning as needed. When this happens, young children are much less likely to find themselves in trouble. Of course none of us can be this patient all the time, but we can do our best and try not to give up. If what is expected only becomes clear to a child *after* they have done something 'wrong', or possibly when they didn't even know what 'wrong' is, it feels confusing, upsetting and unfair — very far from companionable.

But when companions *can* be predictable and are able to explain what is going to happen, it helps babies and young children to feel settled, secure and part of the family. They begin to understand about expectations and behaviour based on knowing what happens, together with a sense of belonging in their family and in their world. What matters is a *combination* of belonging and behaviour.

Chapter 4

Caring Matters

1. How is connecting part of caring?
2. What does companionable caring look like?
3. Are grandparents special companions and carers?
4. How can we choose the best daycare?
5. Changes are upsetting – what can we do?
6. How does caring connect with life-long wellbeing?

1. How is connecting part of caring?

Chapter 3 was about why belonging and behaviour together matters for wellbeing. This chapter is about caring and connecting, not only with other people and especially with companions, but with the whole of the world in which we live. For instance connecting with the natural world is an important part of developing wellbeing, for babies, children and indeed adults. The digital world is increasingly part of the picture too. The innumerable connections that the youngest children make every day, with everything around them, are significantly important for their development.

Very special moments of connection for the youngest children are with their companions. We can see them lighting up. These connections aren't just about talking with them and hearing what they say, although speaking and listening are of course important. It's about body language too. And for the youngest children, connecting is not only about communicating with the people they know and love, but about exploring the world around them, too.

2. What does companionable caring look like?

Regularly providing childcare means there is a lot to think about. As well as the bottom line of eating, sleeping and safety, what important experiences do the youngest children need? Registered daycare providers have to comply with certain standards relating to care, learning and play. The environment must be safe and secure, with activities and play opportunities made available. In daycare settings such as nurseries and childcarers, this provision may or may not be companionable. But while care with family companions at home is not subject to these regulations, the needs of children remain the same. This may feel more challenging for companions who have not experienced the ups and downs of being parents themselves.

Children are learning all the time from everything that happens. They learn from their companions, or indeed from any kind of carers that they are with, and they learn in every situation they are in, companionable or not. We cannot switch off their learning, in much the same way that we cannot switch off their growing (much as we might like to when yet again they need new shoes). They learn from everything that happens to them, wherever they are, from the not-so-good as well as the good. For instance, when at first they cry in their cot and someone comes straight away, they are learning that they are safe and cared about. They learn from experience that there is help at hand when they need it. The cot feels safe. But if they are frequently left when they cry or their companions do not come straight away, they are learning about being on their own with whatever is upsetting them, which is a very different experience. Children who cry at going to nursery may be learning about being on their own in much the same way; or they may stop crying when a companionable carer there swings into action. This is how they learn that nursery is a safe place for them.

These are uncomfortable thoughts, perhaps bringing up times in the past when, if only we had known and were able to, we might have done things differently. But for most people it's safe to say that we were absolutely doing our best at the time, and you can't do more than that. However, what we know now suggests that perhaps doing our best with a companionable approach, as often as we can, is more helpful in the longer term.

The next chapter, Learning Matters, is mainly about positive attitudes to learning. There is a thread running through both these chapters though, about caring, connecting and learning. This is because children's learning attitudes are often unconsciously absorbed from the people and situations around them, rather than as a result of being told things. Later on, when a child is older, how we explain things using language plays an important part, but young children tend to learn not so much from what adults say to them, but from what parents and carers themselves do. For instance, most parents want their children to grow up knowing about right and wrong, sometimes without realising that what they themselves and other carers do is a much more powerful influence on children than what they say. This influence is especially strong when children are being cared for in a companionable way. Small children try very hard to be like the grown-ups that they see often and love the most — their closest companions.

We see them imitating all the time. Take saying 'no' for example. When we say 'no' as little as possible, but always mean it, we can be firm but at the same time friendly and companionable about it. But 'no' doesn't work so well with children whose parents and carers often give in. When the parent's or carer's 'no' hasn't worked, possibly the next step is to resort to threats. And if those don't work perhaps 'time out' and as a last resort a smack. When this happens, children themselves will be learning to say 'no' that way too. If taking no notice of someone, or threatening them, or even hitting is acceptable for grown-ups to do, then it must be acceptable for children too. This sort of embedded early learning, that ignoring, threatening or even hitting are acceptable if nothing else works is unhelpful when children are young, and extremely worrying in older children and adults.

So what does companionable caring look like? It is mostly about relationships between children and their carers. Companionable caring is friendly, affectionate, respectful and often loving, essentially accepting on both sides. Life is usually (but of course not always) relaxed and unhurried. Most important is the way that children and carers listen to each other, sharing good times (and not-so-good) and enjoying each other's company.

3. Are grandparents special companions and carers?

Families with companionable grandparents are particularly fortunate. Grandparents can bring love and security, fun times and sometimes glimpses of past family events and history. Their 'job description', different from that of parents, can vary enormously. Some can quite easily be closely involved while for others, living further away makes the relationship very different. For distant grandparents, these days being able to connect through electronic communication can make such a difference. And if sadly there is a grandparent gap, perhaps another older companion might sometimes not replace, but step into the role.

Many grandparents now are involved in the patchwork of daycare that is often needed when parents are working. For them, it is practical and thoughtful to discuss at the outset how much grandparent commitment is being offered and can realistically be made. Parents can be clear about what help they need most, and then keep a sensitive watch on roughly where everyone is on the line that goes from contented companionship at one end, to despairing exhaustion at the other. Whether grandparents are near or far, there's satisfaction and pleasure in supporting their own children or an extended family in becoming parents, in being open to new ideas, and being happy to talk over everyone's expectations.

Grandparents who anticipate visits or regular times at their home with their grandchild will have consulted parents and may need to take a few important safety precautions. A safety checklist might include items such as putting away precious and poisonous things, installing car restraints for young children, and a safe cot or place to sleep. Later What Matters chapters suggest lots of ways to make the most of this precious time. Caring for small children calls for responsibility and energy and sometimes family companions may need support as well.

4. How can we choose the best daycare?

An immediate question is about *when* you'll need daycare. Most importantly, in terms of developing a baby's wellbeing, is what you decide to do in the first year. In those all-important twelve months a baby's need for caring, consistent and responsive adults is most likely to be met by parents or other companionable carers at home, or perhaps the home of a companionable child-minder.

Finding companionable *centre-based* daycare for the first year, if you can afford it, is more of a challenge. But very many parents now simply cannot afford *not* to return to work, nor to give up the chance of maintaining their career over the longer term. This need to work can, for some, be a source of intense sadness and sometimes destructive guilt. If funded government policies that currently prioritise daycare provision were based on what we know about early child development, the situation might be very different. Granting families access to quality services that focus on parenting and supporting life at home during the early years and enabling parents to choose without penalties when to return to work, would transform outcomes for children, families and the economy. Better solutions to what is, for so many families, such a difficult and distressing situation are long overdue.

But for those who *can* afford it, choosing the best daycare outside the home is all about deciding what matters to you. What do you care about? When you are checking out possible places, your tick list might include questions about whether the place is warmly welcoming, where *everyone* belongs, regardless of background and ethnicity; about staff pay, conditions and continuing professional development; about the toys (a balance between natural materials and plastic?); about the percentage of agency workers, and staff turnover; about efficiency; and about whether the publicity blurb is reflected in reality.

How much time is spent outside? How good is the match between the nursery and your own lives (for instance, generally immaculate, or 'lived in'?). Are parents welcome in the nursery? Do the nursery staff or does the childcarer feel companionable? There are no right answers and only you can find the childcare that works best both for you and for your child.

A nursery that looks tidy and colourful with many lovely toys, that costs a lot and doesn't try to involve you when you don't have time, may tick a lot of boxes and actually be the reassurance that you need. Perhaps you, like many other parents, need to work, especially in the second half of that first year. Or perhaps like many others you really want to be back at work (and you are not alone in this). Only you can decide on what will be right for you and for your child. But if you do need or want to work, and daycare is an option, then when choosing the best nursery for you and your baby or young child, on your tick-list you might have 'emotionally warm and welcoming' as one of the key things you look for.

5. Changes are upsetting – what can we do?

For the youngest children, getting used to changes is what life is all about as they move from womb to world, from cradle to cot, one place to another, one person to another, one group of friends to the next. Comparatively small events in their everyday lives can be traumatic but handling them in a companionable way in the earliest days can help with the bigger changes later, like starting daycare, going to 'big school', moving from primary to secondary school, losing close friends and making new ones, first days at college and work, and so on. It helps when those first daily experiences of change (the different place, the companion's arrival, the new song or game) come to be associated with pleasure. Ways of building babies' and young children's resilience in the face of anticipated change are likely to be based on listening and watching them carefully right from the start and taking their distress seriously, even if we don't understand it.

In times of change, familiar people, places and routines become even more important than usual. Moving house is *not* the moment to buy a new cot or leave the old high chair behind. Or a change in daycare staffing that means new faces for a baby or young child may not be the best time to re-arrange taking and collecting arrangements, if you can avoid it. Essentially, it is about not changing everything at once, but changing as few things at a time as possible. Careful preparatory introductions to new arrangements and new people is a good way to go. The strategy of children knowing what to expect, that helps so much to reduce tantrums, is also hugely helpful in preparing for changes that you know are imminent. Becoming familiar with previously unknown places and people *before* they become a daily reality can make all the difference.

These early experiences will be setting a pattern for the future leading to confidence or anxiety, eager anticipation or dread. It is incredibly hard to persuade a small child, or indeed an adult, that there is no need for anxiety and dread when that child or adult knows from experience what daily anxiety and dread feels like. But to have experienced changes as manageable or even sometimes positive can help a great deal. Changes one at a time mean that we can find ways to make the most of what is left. However, on occasions where everything just has to change at once, for instance a new house, new school, and new friends, then parents and companions who can remain steady and consistent is a great help.

6. How does caring connect with life-long wellbeing?
We are all used to the idea that if we are to look after other people, we need to look after ourselves. This care of 'self' is central to the popular idea of wellbeing. But looking at when people feel contented in real life, an even more important aspect of caring emerges, especially for parents. While we do need to be able to take care of ourselves, it is taking care of others (children, partners, neighbours, people who need us) that gives us the most satisfaction, provided we are not overwhelmed by it and don't neglect our own feelings and needs. This satisfaction in taking care of others can be seen so clearly too in young children's desire to care. Knowing that they have successfully 'helped' gives them enormous satisfaction. Caring for others, even in the smallest of companionable ways, gives children, and many adults if they are not overwhelmed, the most contentment of all.

Chapter 5

Learning Matters

1. How do babies and young children learn?
2. How do we know when they are learning?
3. Can we teach positive learning attitudes?
4. When is the right time to start sharing books?
5. Why is it never too early?
6. Children learn through play? How does that work?
7. Do young children have their own favourite ways of playing?

1. How do babies and young children learn?

Babies and young children learn using all their senses, though which senses get used the most depends on ages and stages of child development. They learn by watching, listening, exploring, experimenting, imitating, concentrating, persisting and asking questions. Playing is their best way of doing all these things in ways that make sense to them. Their 'mistakes' mean that next time they can be better, which is how learning works. Their companions are all-important in their learning. These are the people they know and love best. They are the ones who listen to them carefully, give them confidence to carry on, don't go away when it gets interesting and lend a hand when things get difficult.

Babies' and young children's conversations are essential for early learning. Companionable conversations involve taking it in turns to talk and listen. This process of conversational exchange lies at the heart of life-long learning. Alongside the all-important body language, the essential roots of early communicating lie in babies' babbling (before talking) and toddlers' scribbling (before writing).

Listening comes before reading, in the same way that talking comes before writing. How can children learn to read the words on the page or the screen if they have never heard them? Learning to listen and to speak lays foundations in early childhood for later literacy, when they will read other writers' words, and write their own. Listening and speaking, both out loud and on the page, is partly how we learn about our world. This 'taking it in turns' to talk and listen is companionable learning together.

2. How do we know when they are learning?

They are never not learning! Babies and young children never stop learning, in the same way that they never stop growing. But they may be learning things we would rather they didn't learn. They learn from everything that happens, not all good. If only we could turn off the learning switch until the end of this violent row or that frightening noise, but unfortunately there is no switch. Perhaps a slightly different question might be more useful. Instead of *'When* are they learning?' we might ask *'What* are they learning?' In the early days, companionable learning means that babies and young children enjoy learning together with their companions, an important way to start.

In the twenty-first century, what do children actually *need* to be learning? With a future shrouded in such uncertainty, how can we decide what knowledge they'll need twenty years from now? We have very little idea of what will matter then, but of one thing we can be certain. The twenty-first century pace of change means that today's children will need to keep on learning new things throughout their lives. And lasting positive learning attitudes will make all the difference to success.

3. Can we teach positive learning attitudes?

The wonderful news is that we don't need to. This is because babies from the day they are born already have perfect attitudes to learning. The very youngest children in their first year are observant, attentive, curious, exploratory and experimental. They imitate, concentrate, persist and soon are asking questions. They do all these things completely naturally. They are like avidly curious little learning machines, watching and listening, and exploring with all their senses. They experiment with whatever is to hand, for instance finding out about gravity by holding out bits of food and letting go. Will it go down or up? Does it always go down, every time? Small children are always motivated and engaged in finding out about things, provided those things interest them.

But are small children really good at concentrating and persisting? There is a popular idea that they don't know how to learn until we teach them and that children need to be taught how to concentrate and not give up. But what about the times when we have to drag them away from something they are enjoying, like playing with water in the bath, their favourite TV programme, or the playground? Actually their concentration is excellent, but only so long as it's on something they are interested in. What they find hard is being expected to concentrate on things chosen by us that we want them to learn about, but in which they themselves have no interest.

But again, how many of us adults can honestly say we have learned to concentrate on things we haven't chosen and in which we have no interest or motivation to learn? Why do we expect small children to be better at this than we are? It is a normal part of life eventually to find ways to concentrate for a reasonable time on things that we find boring, but in the early years these inappropriate expectations are likely to close down the precious attitudes to learning that babies are born with. The interminable 'Why?' questions are another feature, though this can sometimes be their way to keep the companionable attention going that they enjoy so much. When it's a genuine 'Why?' question, companions do their best. One child who, instead of 'Why?' always asked 'What because of?' probably got better explanations!

Do these essential positive learning attitudes feature much in schools now? Unfortunately, children are often too busy 'learning' to have time to explore, experiment, learn from their mistakes or finish something however long it takes. Perhaps most concerning of all is the prevailing culture that making mistakes is bad. How can anyone learn from their mistakes, acknowledged to be the basic way that knowledge and understanding goes forward, when both children and teachers are strongly encouraged never to make any, and risk being penalised if they do? The fact is that we all make mistakes and sometimes an apology to a child is wholly appropriate: for instance "I'm sorry I made you stop drawing, you hadn't finished had you? Shall we do lots more drawing tomorrow?" When we apologise and try to make amends, we are showing children something important — that it's all right to make mistakes — and how to apologise and do better next time.

So for companions who understand what competent learners the youngest children are, the question is not 'How can we teach these positive learning attitudes?' but 'How can we make sure that children don't lose them? How can we protect and encourage their watching, listening, exploring, experimenting, making mistakes, imitating, concentrating, persisting and asking questions?' Companionable learning when we genuinely do these things together can be a good solution.

4. When is the right time to start sharing books?
There isn't really a right time for books. It's never too early, but neither is it ever too late. While formally 'learning to read', with phonics and reading programmes, is definitely better later on, in early childhood it's all about giving babies and young children a lasting love of books.

Never too early (so right from the start) is wonderful. Sharing books with babies from the beginning is about a combination of security, cuddles and fun. They soon love looking at pictures and hearing our voices. Even if they are not quite there yet with understanding what you are saying, they will learn from the very earliest weeks to associate the feel, look and smell of new books with pleasure in your company. This might be a shameless bit of conditioning, but surely worth it! Chatting about the pictures is easy, and in our possibly exhausted state we can talk away without having to think of things to talk about, partly because the picture book does that for us. Cuddling up with a book helps with that sense of belonging too, and soon (if you are reading mutual old favourites over and over) with knowing what comes next: when to turn the page, knowing what's on the next page, seeing the funny bit coming. And then there will be important decisions for the small child. Which book? Which companion for story time?

5. Why is it never too early?

One reason for getting language going as soon as possible relates to tantrums. The sooner children begin to talk about what they want and how they feel, the fewer the tantrums. Knowing what is coming next gives babies and young children a sense of control, helping too with their frustrating but determined struggle for independence.

It's never too early for decisions either, about what is going to happen. When a small child is offered a choice, for instance about which book to read together, or whether to play outside or stay indoors with us, the choice may not be as straightforward as it sounds. It depends how they hear the question. Some children simply ask themselves "What do I want?" and go ahead and choose. But for others, the question they ask themselves is not "What do I want?" but "What do they want me to say?"

Children who have learned to guess the 'right' answer are hoping for approval, especially if approval is sometimes in doubt. They are becoming dependent on other people's acceptance and approval, for their own security and satisfaction. But being dependent on others' approval can cause problems later, in adolescence and into adulthood. Relationships, behaviour and learning may all be affected, leading to concerning vulnerability. Early opportunities to decide for themselves are precious and something that companions can give children right from the start. A child will be less vulnerable to needing acceptance and approval if they have experienced those things already in a warm, trusting relationship.

6. Children learn through play? How does that work?

One of the universal difficulties for adults about playing with babies and very young children is that most of us remember little of our early days before we were three, and what they felt like. Another difficulty for many of us is finding enough time for children to play as long as they like, until they are finished. We are often in such a hurry these days that this can be a real challenge. Perhaps deliberately companionable days might be a good way of slowing down.

At the start, babies' favourite things to play with, their best 'toys', are us. As well as liking us being with them, they love it when we let them literally play with us, so that they can explore to their hearts' content. Our knuckles make such good teething rings, adults make much funnier noises than any rattle, and almost immediately babies learn that they can lead the way. For instance when they smile, we will smile back and when they bang with their hands, so (gently) do we. It is the baby who takes charge.

Slightly older children need to take charge even more as they play. We might call the sort of play that they need most, 'wellbeing play'. Here is what wellbeing play looks like. It is based on their experiences, pretending around things that they already know about. When they are pretending, children make up their own rules, so they are in control. And they choose what it's about and how it goes, that's not up to us. (Though we can make their choosing easier by the range of what we offer them to play with.) In this kind of play they often pretend things about their future, or about being like us. Sometimes they want to play like this on their own. We can stick around, but only join in if we are invited. (Of course there have to be boundaries to their being in charge, around safety for everyone.)

Young children need plenty of time and enough space to play like this, indoors or out. It involves their ideas and feelings, coordination and thinking skills. It helps them to make sense of their family, their friends and their world. There's no right ending and no hurry. Overall, this kind of 'pretending' wellbeing play is profoundly satisfying for them. The children themselves need to take charge, even if we have been invited to join in. We need to be careful that we don't influence their play without realising what we are doing, getting too involved and starting to take over. Taking over puts us in charge instead of them and might be great fun all round, but it is a different kind of play.

7. Do young children have their own favourite ways of playing?

Yes they do, often based on their thinking patterns (known as schemas). The philosopher, Immanuel Kant, wrote about the idea of schemas 250 years ago. Psychologists and educators have continued to explore this idea, making it increasingly understandable and relevant to our lives with children.

These patterns ebb and flow, remaining with us in various ways all our lives. We are born with them. They may be why sometimes children's enthusiasms can be difficult to manage but play patterns (their schemas) can't be turned off, in the same way that we can't turn off their growing or their learning. These patterns are part of who they are.

Sometimes a pattern seems very strong in a child, and we can see it in how they play. At other times patterns seem to fade, vary in strength, or be joined or even replaced by a different one. Here are some of the most frequent and noticeable patterns (schemas) in early childhood: round and round (rotation); covering up and putting things inside (enveloping and containing); joining things together (connecting); carrying things around (transporting); and jumping, hitting, throwing, shooting, running (trajectory). This last pattern, trajectory, is about anything that involves a moving arc.

These patterns sometimes cause havoc in everyday life at home. Many children have an urgent need to throw, jump, shoot and so on, to hide things somewhere inside, or stick things together. Some children love the process of moving toys and furniture from one place to another, seemingly not at all interested in where it all ends up. Doing these things sometimes gets small children into trouble, and yet they seem unable to stop for long. Playing like this in favourite ways can be very satisfying though. Being a companion gives us great opportunities to notice and nurture children's patterns which are often so important to them. And these patterns don't have to cause havoc if we understand them. It helps to try noticing your child's patterns and then saying 'yes' rather than 'no'. We can then 'feed' them activities that are less liable to cause chaos.

Masking tape, building blocks, Lego and train track keep 'connectors' happy. Cardboard boxes for dens, and blankets and old paper for wrapping are great for 'enclosers'. Anything involving stirring and circles will fascinate a 'round and round' child. Wonderful for 'trajectory' children are hosepipes and other water play, throwing games using paper aeroplanes and beanbags etc., football, cardboard tubes from the recycling for hitting games. And, for these children, always the playground.

These last ideas are especially worth pursuing since throwing, running and jumping etc. can be so disruptive in small home spaces. Bags, baskets, rucksacks and collections of smallish objects will keep the 'transporting' children happy for hours while they play moving house or postperson. With companionable watching and a little ingenuity the possibilities are endless. Happily, there is hardly ever any need to buy toys for these patterns, because everyday real-life things work best, provided they are safe.

Most of us enjoy doing the things that interest us; often the things that fit with our own habitual 'patterns' as adults. Knowing about these patterns can help us to understand ourselves, as well as children and other adults. They illuminate how we think, our interests and satisfactions, new activities we might enjoy, even the presents we might like. And they can help us to understand young children, to enjoy them, and to make the most of our time with them.

This chapter is all about companionable early learning; about how and when it starts, about books for babies, and about young children deciding things and being safely in control. Most importantly it is about how they learn when they play in particular ways, and about their play patterns. Babies and young children experiencing these kinds of satisfying playtimes, especially during the first three to four years, are laying down the foundations for contented life-long learning.

Chapter 6

Doing Matters

1. What can we do with the youngest children?
2. Don't we need training?
3. What does the natural world mean for children?
4. Why do they always want to help?
5. Is there a right way to share books with a small child?
6. What is 'old friends' about – is this bit just for grandparents?
7. Does food with small children have to be a battlefield?
8. Does going out matter?
9. Does playing count as something that matters?
10. What about screens, are they bad for young children?
11. What's the hurry?

1. What can we do with the youngest children?

The youngest children find out about their world mostly by doing things and watching what happens, rather than by being told. Here are some starting points, not as a 'to do' list with instructions but offered as illustrations of the sorts of ways to be involved in companionable and satisfying activities with young children. This chapter includes practical ideas about helping, sharing books, old friends, food, going out, playing, screens, and slowing down.

2. Don't we need training?

We may have ideas about *what* to do, but *how* can we do things with children in ways that work *for them*? If we care about knowing what matters for babies and young children, don't we need training of some sort? How do we choose the right training? Answers to these important questions are perhaps both unexpected and reassuring. Essentially we find out what to do with very young children by making some decisions about what matters to us, and then by doing, watching and listening. When we are attentive with babies and young children, when we watch and listen to other companions, and when we use our curiosity to find out about things with them, we gradually learn what they need.

Parents or primary carers are usually the ones who will know their child best and are most important. It's essential for all other companions to check in regularly with them and with each other, honestly sharing problems and challenges as well as joys and achievements. These conversations will make an enormous difference to babies' and young children's security.

It may be that we don't all agree about what matters. Yet even babies very soon understand which of their companions minds about what. In cases where there is very fundamental disagreement about what matters, companions will need to turn to parents themselves as the final arbiters; or withdraw for the time being. Listening to other children's companions, other families, and useful advice based on trustworthy evidence can be helpful too, in deciding what matters to us. And then it is a case of 'learning by doing', with the children themselves as teachers. When we are responding to them, it is as if they are training us in the particular kinds of caring that they need.

3. What does the natural world mean for children?

Young children start to form a sense of their own identity and understand how they fit into their world from an early age. Many of us live in cities, in centrally heated homes, eating mainly processed food. In seeing ourselves as separate from nature, maybe even in control of it, we are not helping children to experience the awe, wonder and fascination that is all around them. Going outside whenever we can really matters, even just around the corner or down the road. We can use all our senses not just to see but to listen, touch, smell and even (cautiously) taste, to explore and connect with nature. Young children delight in exploring this wonderful natural world into which they have been born. Small scale is best, with leaves, single flowers, tiny insects. With a magnifying glass or bug bottle in pocket or bag, going out can suddenly become a thrilling, magical, companionable experience.

Connecting with nature matters so much for children; for their curiosity, their belonging and their learning, and for their health. And as companions we can *genuinely* explore nature with them. Small children are fortunate when they have at least one companion to share the delight, excitement and mystery of the natural world we live in. We can help them to see how much we depend on the living world of plants and creatures. Learning in childhood to care for things in nature can sow the seeds of responsibility for the planet, so urgently needed now in the twenty-first century.

4. Why do they always want to help?

When small children help us, they get to learn about what grown-ups do. This matters a lot to them because they want to be like us. It's often about what happens at home. Preparing the meals, and the cleaning, cooking, washing and shopping often fascinates them. This is what forms the basis of their later learning. We all learn in a kind of spiral and helping can be part of the spiral. As time passes, with every new curve we revisit our previous learning at another level. At this early stage we are simply joining small children in beginning to find out about their world, especially things in it that interest them most.

From all this homely helping with companions that they love to imitate, can come their wish to read and write like them, laying the foundations of their later more formalised understanding of mathematics, chemistry and physics, biology, geography and history, of literature and the arts. 'Helping' is a great way to learn about their family, their home and their world, linking naturally with the other most important way they learn, by playing.

'Helping' guarantees being together too; always a winner for a small child. These days we tend to think of household chores as tedious, to be got out of the way as quickly as possible. Small children take the opposite view though. What could be more fun than sorting out the laundry basket with you and loading the washing machine, adding the soap and, for some 'round and round' children, watching the washing going round and round? This is doing important things, together with a precious companion. There are so many favourite activities: all sorts of cleaning of course (dusting, sweeping, polishing etc.); sorting things like spoons and forks; putting away clean clothes (especially socks) and toys; clearing out a low-down cupboard. 'Helping' is not unlike having a little apprentice about the place. And it means that you can get on with things that need doing, together.

Mending and fixing things is great for children who are really keen to help. Any time someone in the family gets out the tools, perhaps to mend something precious, sort out a door frame or fix broken shelves, clean out the car or mend a bike, "Can I help?" is likely to be heard. It's often not so much that they want to use the grown-up saw or the pliers, more that they know if they are helping with real tools, they'll definitely have your attention, and they'll be doing a real grown-up job with you, the right way. Though your heart might sink when the flat pack arrives, your child will be happy to help you for hours, not as a spectator but busy sorting and counting out screws, passing you the instructions and holding things steady!

Of course a small child seriously slows things down, but does that matter so much in the course of a companionable day? When children ask, "Can I help?" they are asking for something very important.

5. Is there a right way to share books with a small child?

There's no right way. It depends on working out together, by trial and error, how to get it right with this particular baby or small child. It's about deciding together the ways that work for *you*. These favourite companionable situations can be a major source of pleasure and satisfaction. How familiar is the often bossy, relentless and sometimes puzzling request to "read it!". Often this is not so much about the book itself, but about a child needing their companion to stay put. Children learn very quickly what works to 'anchor' their companions. If 'anchoring' is what they need, then books and stories are often the perfect answer.

When and where works best? Any time, and almost anywhere, probably! For one boy, a long bath time was good for stories, though bedtime stories are usually best in bed. But how about taking a book or two on a bus or train, out in the garden, or to the park? A car, a cot or highchair can work, though it helps to find somewhere that's comfortable for companions too.

What sort of books are best? At least sometimes it's worth choosing ones that we will enjoy reading and playing with too. There are so many wonderful books to choose from: nursery rhyme books, animal books, pop-up books, picture books, board books, counting books, funny books, bath books, fairy tale books, song books, bedtime books. The choice is amazing right from the start for babies, and just gets better and better.

Happily, good children's books are now readily available and amazingly cheap. You can buy several for the price of a take-away pizza; and they last longer! As well as bookshops, many supermarkets now sell children's books. Best of all for embryonic avid readers with limited budgets, is the amazing choice and availability that comes free from precious public libraries. Borrowing from the library is a great way to try out different sorts of books and discover favourite authors. It also has the advantage of being a reason for a little expedition. Once a book becomes a lasting favourite though, you may want to buy a copy if you can, to keep.

6. What is 'old friends' about – is this bit just for grandparents?

'Old friends' here does *include* grandparents, but it also means much-loved things and familiar activities. As well as people, this is about deeply familiar toys and precious objects, books and stories, songs, rhymes and music. We sometimes assume that children will be bored unless something new is happening. But old friends in the wider sense often come high up on children's 'trueloves' lists.

Songs and rhymes have the same familiar predictability that children so often enjoy with favourite books. Knowing what comes next gives them a sense of control. It's useful to collect in our heads a few songs and rhymes we know so well that we don't even have to think about them. There is evidence that children who are familiar with songs and rhymes in early childhood are likely to be good readers later on. One or two favourite books can always be with us too, even on the bus or in the park, and can sometimes be a better source of comfort and distraction than any number of toys.

For many fortunate children, old friends do include grandparents and other older family companions. Sometimes it's easier for an older generation to give companionable attention. They may not be having to juggle quite so many things, in the way that parents do. This is one of the best things about being a grandparent, because companionable attention is exactly what young children want from us most.

Certain special words or phrases can become old friends too. These are words for children's ears, rather than ours (although probably we like hearing them too). It helps when we get into the habit of saying these gentle, reassuring kinds of words to children as often as possible: "I'm just here", "I see you", "Yes",

"Thank you", "This is what's going to happen", "I'm sorry", "No rush", "You did it!"

7. Does food with small children have to be a battlefield?

Not necessarily. In fact anything to do with food and helping usually works well with small children. Growing things to eat, buying, cooking, eating, and clearing up all work with companions together. These routines that underpin pleasurable eating can help a lot. What children eat, and where their food comes from, is probably one of the most fascinating aspects of their early childhood. From breast or bottle to discovering what their favourite meals are made of and where the ingredients came from, to how to unwrap things or cook them; and from laying the table to clearing up, young children are usually deeply interested in being involved. The satisfaction is not necessarily automatic, though. It is less a question of *what* they are doing, more about the companionable *ways* in which these things can be done together.

Cooking together is an all-time favourite with small children. But when we launch into a cooking session (making fairy cakes perhaps, or little pizzas) we may be heading for sticky fingers everywhere, a generous sprinkling of every ingredient on the kitchen floor, and piles of clothes washing and dirty dishes. Though a special treat for children, this is enough to put most adults off; but cooking doesn't have to be sticky and chaotic. Small children can help to prepare a meal by washing vegetables and fruit, counting out cutlery (one for me, one for you), putting food on plates and dishes, calling people when it's ready.

So although children love the satisfaction of real cooking, perhaps putting something in the oven and bringing it out again twenty minutes later when it's cooked (just enough time for a story) very little children are perfectly happy with a much simpler version. Supposing the meal is baked beans on toast with carrot and cucumber sticks, followed by a satsuma and two small biscuits, there are many ways they can help with that.

Laying the table is full of possibilities, too. What with counting up how many people will be eating, finding the right number of the cutlery and plates, collecting things to drink out of, and putting it all on the table in the right place, there is so much to think and talk about. It's a series of satisfying, companionable tasks that companions and children can do together.

Table manners can be an issue with young children, but this is often because we expect good manners too young, before children have had enough opportunities to understand. Basically, good manners are about fitting in with the people around us and thinking about them enough to know we are not upsetting them. Perhaps one thing to bear in mind is the way young children can learn good manners from us, in a 'caught not taught' way. When they are old enough (developmentally able) they will automatically pick up from us how we eat meals with them. Setting them an example with the behaviour we would like to see is so much more effective and lasting than just telling them how we would like them to behave.

When companions and children sit down to eat *together*, even if it's only two of us, we are, for the duration of the meal, anchored. Unhurried mealtimes are not only better for the digestion, but they are also times when everyone can listen, think and talk together. Doing this as often as possible goes a long way to making meals with small children a pleasure.

8. Does going out matter?

There are so many good reasons for going out with small children. Gardening with them can be very special and for families fortunate enough to have a little space somewhere outside, with a few grow bags there are many possibilities. Being a bit patient and not too ambitious is useful when growing things to eat, and the sense of anticipation, awe and wonder help a lot through the waiting periods. A minor harvest of herbs and mustard-and-cress can be grown on a windowsill; and bean sprouts are easy and cheap if there is space in a warm, dark cupboard. Children love talking about what they are doing and learning how to do it properly. Feeling the achievement of having helped to grow something that everyone can eat is very special. And if you are not (yet) a gardener, best of all is when you are both learning how to grow these things successfully, together.

Continuing with the food theme, eating outside can be a big treat. A picnic need not involve a major expedition though. Just stepping out into the garden or a nearby park with a snack works well. In changeable or cold weather, eating just outside the house or flat means it's easy to run for cover. With this approach, picnics don't need to involve a lot of preparation, and can happen quite easily. Younger children, who especially need to be safe, will be happy sitting in their pushchair to eat, or close to people on a rug. Older children may want to wander around while they munch. Of course that is only fine if they are safe, which brings in the need for family rules. Eating when we are out is great for companionable talking together; there are lots of things to talk about, and usually plenty of time.

Going out generally with young children these days though, is liable to be fraught with worries. There could be dangerous traffic, strangers, children's behaviour (both our children and others) and so on. But in spite of the consequent restrictions for children it's still, for them, definitely worth it. When we take responsibility for children away from home, it means we can never take our eyes off them, and this is exactly what they love! As well as frequent changes of scene and the chance to let off steam that young children often need, this may be one reason they always seem to love going out.

A key part of going out is how we get there. "Are we walking?" "Where's the pushchair?" "Lost the car keys!" "Hurry up, we'll miss the bus." "We mustn't be late for the train." The decision about how to get there is usually to do with what's easiest, quickest or cheapest, but sometimes, if there's a choice, it might be worth choosing what's healthiest, more fun, or perhaps better for the planet.

Going out doesn't have to mean a major journey though. It can simply be fetching something from the garden or going as far as the corner of the street. Here are some small expeditions for very young children: bringing in the washing; walking to the corner and back; going to a nearby shop; a trip to the local park; dropping off and picking up older children from school; visiting other people's houses; going to a local group; or the nearest library. When these often brief times outside are companionable, they can be completely satisfying. Although we sometimes wonder why we bothered, the wellbeing value of going out lies as much in just managing to get out and come home again, as it does with the destination.

9. Does playing count as something that matters?

Even quite recently, people thought that 'just playing' was a time wasting alternative to the more important activities of 'learning' and 'work'. These days, play is still often seen as all about physical wellbeing. After a spell of 'work', we talk about children needing to go outside to play. Children's physical development is, of course, extremely important. Being able to get around, maybe by crawling, then walking, then running and jumping, opens up new worlds to them. Many of them work incredibly hard at these skills, with tremendous determination. Their physical confidence, or maybe lack of it, makes a big difference to their play with other children and to our expectations of them.

When children play in their own ways, with and about the people in their lives, about their experiences, their interests and enthusiasms, they are learning. Even the very youngest children often play in this way with their companions and the things with which they have become closely familiar. What do children need for this kind of play? They need their companions to be around, attentive and available if needed, but not in control. The limited authority that children experience most of the time in real life is, appropriately, very much weighted on the side of adults. But in 'pretending' wellbeing play it is the other way around. Children are the ones who decide, and it is up to their adult companions to allow them (within the boundaries of safety, not hurting anyone etc.). This way children have the freedom to arrange things in their own way for a change. It is how they often replay events in their lives, learning to make sense of them.

Helping children to play like this involves letting them play with real-life things. But (unlike 'helping' situations where you are very much in control), now they mustn't have anything that might break or hurt them. However there are many things that will work for them. For kitchen play there are light saucepans, wooden spoons, plastic cups and bowls, perhaps a few ordinary biscuits. Instead of the real cooker, washing machine or dishwasher, big cardboard boxes are the way to go. Up-end them, draw cooking rings on the top, or cut a round door in the side. For the bathroom, a box with an empty bowl, mug, toothbrush and towel, and for the bedroom a folded up rug and a cushion on the floor in the corner. These things work very well for pretending. And because children will be playing about situations in real life as they know it, home-made things that we have made together will usually be more satisfying than expensive plastic toys that cannot convincingly be changed into other things the children are imagining — perhaps a shop, or a doctor's or dentist's room.

10. What about screens, are they bad for young children?

This is a fraught and difficult topic for many people, often generating judgmental responses that can be very upsetting.

It is included here with some caution, touching on frequent questions and outlining current evidence. Many of us happily lend a smartphone or tablet to our little ones, they look so cute and fascinated, how can it do any harm?

But how much screen time might be too much? What are the pros and cons? What do companions need to know about children and screens? Decades of research shows both positive and negative developmental outcomes, and more evidence into definitive effects on the youngest children of this ever-changing aspect of our lives is urgently needed. What is already clear is that children's screen time activities and habits get established early on. So 'Are screens bad for young children?' is a valid and important but perhaps over simple question. We need more evidence to know the answer. It's safe to say though, that babies under a year old do not learn from machines. They learn from real life, with real people.

Watching television is often promoted as good for children's developing language, but this only relates to half the process: the benefits of hearing speech, but not of using it. Children learn to speak by speaking. There are concerns about a lot of TV watching in the early years, mainly for three reasons. First, the effect on long-term health problems such as obesity. Second, increased aggression through seeing violence as normal. And third, children's vulnerability to manipulative advertising. There is general agreement that it's better when adults can watch companionably with children and talk together about what they are seeing.

What about the benefits of screens? Although the youngest children do better with real conversations, there's no doubt that early familiarity and competence with digital technology will serve them well in the future. And we adults may understandably depend on children's screen time to some extent, to give us a break when we need it. If you are worried about this, here are some questions that might help:

- Is what your child is seeing age-appropriate?
- Do you try and watch together, at least some of the time?
- Do you make sure there's a balance between time on screens and time in real life?
- Do you always turn off at meal times so you can talk with each other?

And last, there is evidence that getting enough sleep matters for young children, and that looking at screens at bedtime can interfere with their sleep. So:

- Do you make sure screens are off, *well* before bedtime?

11. What's the hurry?

Many adults say how much they need a little time and space of their own. Children need their own time and space too. When young children set the pace, it is different from our own: slower, and with a great deal of watching, thinking and questioning. Most of us know what it feels like, not to have a moment to ourselves all day. When a lot is happening for us, we need time to think things over, to try and figure out what they mean, to make sense of it all. For small children, a lot is happening for them all the time, partly because they absorb everything that is going on around them, not yet having learned to be selective. Life, for them, can be a relentless stream of situations, experiences, people and expectations.

These days we try to cram so much into every day. Perhaps we are afraid that the children will get bored and might cause trouble if there is not something going on all the time. Or perhaps it is we ourselves who find the idea of time to spare so difficult. Children need time for their growing independence too, for instance when they are learning to get themselves dressed, or to find something they've lost, or simply to keep on trying. And just as children need mental space, like us they need a little physical space they can call their own as well. These physical spaces may simply be a baby's own cot, their pushchair, or a shelf where they keep their own things; spaces that they know really do belong to them. When companions respect children's needs in this way, then children learn about respecting others' needs too.

All the sections in this chapter are about examples of themes in other chapters. Children can thrive and have fun helping, sharing and playing with the people they know and love best, doing things that matter.

Chapter 7

You Matter

1. Isn't it the baby that matters?
2. How can I make things better, for me?
3. From symptoms to causes: what's the problem?
4. When a problem won't shift, what can I do?
5. What's normal?
6. And what's *good enough*?

1. Isn't it the baby that matters?

This chapter is mostly for mothers and other primary carers. It is especially for mothers who have just given birth to a new baby (or babies) though it may help for other companions to read it too, especially partners. Much of it may strike a chord with other companions, especially those who do a lot of caring, or who are not used to caring. Many parents and carers will be doing fine and probably don't need to read this chapter. However, 'doing fine' comes and goes, so you might want to remember that 'You Matter' is here, just in case. Others may be feeling they are struggling, given the inevitable challenges of this time. Absolutely no-one should feel bad about struggling, and perhaps there is something in what follows that might help.

Mothers with their first baby sometimes feel a kind of identity crisis; who am I, now? You matter so much to your baby, your partner, your family and closest friends; but do you matter to yourself? How is your confidence? In this new identity of 'mother' which can be tied up with pain, exhaustion and inexperience, your inner self confidence may have taken a knock. Perhaps you can't see what a great job you are doing in this incredibly challenging situation and in your heart there is that conviction, at least some of the time, that you are a terrible mother? If so, you are not alone in this. Many new parents are quite uncertain about their own wellbeing; they are no longer sure that they feel well in themselves and in their dealings with other people, and they experience doubts about their ability to cope.

In all families, the levels of wellbeing ebb and flow like the tide on a beach. Most of the time the upsides are there to hold on to like lifebelts, if you can manage it. But occasionally, in difficult times, there is a feeling that nothing can be done and it is simply a case of sitting it out. And this may well be right. But if this happens and you are feeling really low, looking after yourself is essential; for your own wellbeing and, because you are at the heart of things just now, for the whole family too.

2. How can I make things better, for me?

Here are some cautious wellbeing questions and suggestions that are about looking after yourself:

- Are you eating enough, and is what you are eating good for you? Try not to skip meals or rely on snacks, especially if you are breast feeding. Maybe there is someone around who can help by looking out for you and perhaps bring you meals sometimes?
- If you have older children, can you manage to be careful about how *they* are eating? While we know there is a direct link between sugar intake and behaviour, in the current economic circumstances it may be difficult to avoid cheap food which often contains more sugar. But if you are able to avoid them eating quite so much of it, your own life just might be a little easier.
- If you're on your own with the baby, it may help if there is someone who is often around that you can trust, and who really cares about you and the baby. If not, you might try

looking around for possible people who could help you from time to time; people are often very willing to help when they know you need them.

- Social media can be a huge source of help, advice and connection, just when you need it most. But it can also get between you and your baby and sometimes have a negative effect by feeding you stories of perfect parenting that are totally unrealistic. Can you use the help it offers while avoiding the elements that will wind you up?

- Exercise is good for mental as well as physical health, so it's worth trying to fit in some sort of exercise occasionally, such as a walk in your neighbourhood.

- Can you give yourself a little time and space somehow? Maybe you could take a long bath or shower or arrange to go out for a little while.

- Slow down. You can't do everything, and perhaps some things don't really matter so much right now? Do you really need to get that laundry/washing up/hoovering done today, or would it be better to rest yourself?

- Be honest with yourself about how you're *really* feeling and share with others. If you're tired and stressed it's best not to bottle things up.

- Is there a way you could get one good night's sleep? If this question makes you want to scream or cry, it matters.

- Keep in touch with your friends. If, deep down, you know you need help, try and get it quickly.

- Occasionally, learn something new no matter how small, that is not directly related to children and families.

- Make the most of absolutely all help that comes your way.

Even one or two of these things might help, but maybe nothing does. One thing is certain though. With young children a problem almost never lasts very long. While there will probably be another to take its place, at least it will be different.

3. From symptoms to causes: what's the problem?

Unfortunately there are few quick fixes for coping with difficult times. When something goes wrong, our first thought is usually about what needs doing to fix it; or at least to manage it. We probably see (or hear) the *symptoms* of the problem very clearly; for instance the baby is wailing, or we are weeping.

We recognise these symptoms, but we need to identify the cause. We get better and better at soothing and comforting our children (and perhaps other companions) but unless we identify what the fundamental problem is, the effect of cuddles and comfort may only be short term. A relentless underlying cause of problems in many families is financial instability. While it is parents and carers feeling this stress, often babies and small children sense it. Even if you are stuck in this situation for now, perhaps it helps to acknowledge that when anyone in the family feels stress, it is possible that it is actually being felt by everyone, even in very subtle ways. That this is how stress works cannot be helped, it just is. That our brains and emotions respond in this way is no-one's fault, *especially* not yours.

4. When a problem won't shift, what can I do?

To start with, it's a case of putting your finger on what's concerning you. For instance, you may be concerned about whether your baby is feeding properly and gaining enough weight. This is a problem with a range of possible factors. So break the problem down into manageable chunks. Make a plan to tackle one aspect of it at a time (and not starting with the hardest). That way you begin to feel you are making progress and are less likely to feel totally overwhelmed. Remember that success breeds success.

If that doesn't solve it, giving yourself a break from the problem can help. This is important, especially if you feel like you are on a treadmill dealing with a child (or even another adult) and you seem to be going round and round with the problem, getting nowhere and are tired of thinking about it. It can help to first write down on a piece of paper what the problem is, how often it happens, where, when and who — in fact everything about it, so that you have an accurate record. Then, (providing the problem is not urgent), you can put the paper in a safe place and a reminder on the calendar for when to get it out again (and where you put it!). At least you've done something. And in the meantime, remembering to say "yes" as often as you can (and "no" when you must) to the child or adult concerned is sometimes helpful.

When the date arrives, you can get the paper out again and have a fresh think. Often by then things will be much better; and if they are not, at least you will have an account of what the problem is, and how long it has been going on. This can be especially useful if the next thing you need to do is to seek help.

5. What's normal?

Becoming a mother can be a bit like finding yourself in a tumble dryer of emotions whirling relentlessly round and round. The amazing joy and wonder are usually all mixed up with pain, exhaustion, anxiety, doubt, guilt and depression. Boredom and loneliness may not be far away and at first you hardly know which way is up. All of these feelings are a very normal reaction to your physical state and to finding yourself suddenly in charge of a precious and completely helpless new life.

No matter how many books you may or may not have read and hours you may have spent listening to people telling you how to do it and that you will be fine, it may not feel like that. Just as it's normal for babies to cry, it's normal for parents to feel anxious. But there is a fine line between normal anxiety and postnatal depression. If you think you may be suffering with the latter (it is very common) talk with your doctor, midwife or health visitor as soon as possible, to access the support you need.

6. And what's *good enough?*

What if you can't immediately stop the crying, you forget something, or just somehow feel you must be doing it all wrong? What if you are convinced you are a bad parent? Feeling exhausted doesn't help. The more you worry about getting things wrong, the more likely you are to start feeling guilty about everything. But if we were hoping to be perfect, we can forget it because no-one is. In spite of the pain and desperate tiredness, instead of guilt we can try hanging on to the joy and wonder moments. Deciding what matters to you will help you to be a contented *good enough* companion.

Chapter 8

Looking Ahead

1. Toddlers grow into teenagers
2. The teenage roller-coaster
3. Wellbeing for life?
4. Making a difference to families and communities?

This book is about making the most of our lives with young children now, in these first few years. But looking ahead to when these same children are in their teens, their twenties, perhaps even parents themselves, will all this have made any difference?

1. Toddlers grow into teenagers

Toddlers and teenagers have something in common that preoccupies them both and tends to influence everything they do. At both these stages of their lives they are significantly dependent for survival on the people who provide and care for them. But also at these stages they are struggling to gain independence from these same people. Of course children aged between 5–12 years are dependent too, but generally at that stage they are more interested in the 'right' way to do things, in order to belong and fit in.

The potential battlegrounds of life with both toddlers and teenagers are mostly characterised by very high levels of frustration. The frustrations that toddlers experience and the frustrations that teenagers feel have much in common. So laying positive and lasting foundations about managing frustration at the toddler stage (belonging-and-boundaries, saying yes, and so on) may well turn out to have been helpful, once those toddlers are teenagers.

Feeling safe and secure matters throughout life, not just in childhood. Young children's feelings of safety and security come from the way companions deliberately nurture their sense of belonging and pay attention to their fears in the early years. The other side of the belonging-and-boundaries coin involves the expectations about behaviour that are a consequence of belonging. It can be very helpful when young people understand this too. Families and companions who have made a *lasting* habit of saying yes as often as possible and saying no firmly on the occasions when it's really needed, know that fewer frustrations come along.

2. The teenage roller-coaster

Teenagers are subject to extremely unsettling changes, physically, emotionally and socially. During this period there are likely to be plenty of difficult times mixed in with the good. Most young people manage to survive these challenges, though they are hanging on for dear life to the roller-coaster of adolescence, ranging from peaks of high hope and happiness to troughs of depression and despair. For some teenagers, the challenges are just about manageable. But for others, their lives may become a catalogue of disasters, real or imagined, sometimes leading to long term physical or mental illness. How can these teenage dangers be minimised?

Experiences in the earliest years lay down the foundations for everything to come. Our understanding of the common ground between very young children and teenagers indicates that, looking ahead, it makes sense to invest in child development in the earliest years. And this means not only families looking at family life in this way, but a wide range of government departments and services engaging with it too.

3. Wellbeing for life?

Looking ahead to their twenties and thirties, by then will those early foundations be making a difference to levels of wellbeing, health and happiness? Having positive attitudes to learning will surely be extraordinarily useful in making the most of life, especially when the future is so uncertain. There may be apprenticeships, college or university courses, new jobs, colleagues and places to live and work. Valuing old friends while making new ones is precious, and so is knowing how to slow down when life becomes too hectic. That confidence in themselves, rooted in their experiences of taking their own decisions and making things happen, is often vital during their twenties and thirties. And what about parenting? Perhaps this could be a generational approach, coming full circle?

4. Making a difference to families and communities?

This possibility of making a wider difference seems especially relevant at this time. The underlying sense of direction in What Matters is about our need for connection. It is about learning how we connect with others; to support each other, to learn and to be together. So many factors in our world just now go against this kind of caring connection. Pandemics, migrations, wars, increasing anxieties and fears often seem to be actively keeping us apart.

Evidence suggests that these caring connections might be protected and extended if governments *effectively* prioritise and celebrate early childhood, families and communities. The possibility of significantly positive results opens up. Studies show that to reach their *full* potential, children need to be well nourished and cared for, stimulated, nurtured and protected from stress *from the time their lives begin*. Government support early in their lives is key to setting them on a higher development trajectory. And *early* government investments have higher rates of return than most remedial later-life ones, as well as the potential to increase returns to other future investments in these children.

These findings in relation to the developmental needs of children themselves (not simply focusing on quantity and quality in childcare provision outside the home) are surely highly thought-provoking for governments willing to acknowledge them. Here are solutions for governments to explore, and not only in relation to medium and long term financial stability and positive impacts on the work force. The physical and mental health, as well as the social, emotional and cognitive development of newborn citizens is now undermined in so many ways. Thinking about What Matters in families with the youngest children is more urgent than ever. Perhaps this might be a way to turn the tide back towards stronger wellbeing, mental health and happiness for all.

Together, in families and in communities, a companionable approach can surely make a positive difference. This way, there can be so much more confidence, collaboration and determination to find better ways to care for each other and for the natural world. As we look ahead, what matters more than that?

O-BOOKS

SPIRITUALITY

O-Books is a leading publisher of Body, Mind, and Spirit books. We publish spirituality, personal development, and self-help titles, working in partnership with authors to produce authoritative and innovative books. Our authors offer wisdom from ancient teachings, with new perspectives and interpretations. O-Books aim to enlighten and inspire our readers.

Recent bestsellers from O-Books are:

Awakening Child
A journey of inner transformation through teaching your child mindfulness and compassion.
Heather Grace MacKenzie
Paperback: 978-1-78535-408-3 ebook: 978-1-78535-409-0

A Colourful Dose of Optimism
Prescribe your own Happy Colours to Feel Good NOW
Jules Standish
It's time for us to look on the bright side, by boosting our mood and lifting our spirit, both in our interiors, as well as our closet.
Paperback: 978-1-78904-927-5 ebook: 978-1-78904-928-2

Natural Happiness
Use Organic Gardening Skills to Cultivate Yourself
Alan Heeks
Deepen your roots to grow through uncertainty.
Paperback: 978-1-80341-496-6 ebook: 978-1-80341-497-3

Daylight Saving Time
The Power of Growing Older
David W. Berner
Daylight Saving Time: Facing age with grace and mindfulness.
Paperback: 978-1-80341-511-6 ebook: 978-1-80341-520-8

Generation Panic
Simple & Empowering Techniques to Combat Anxiety
Agi Heale
Generation Panic is a one-stop shop with over
100 tips and techniques to help busy
professionals combat anxiety.
Paperback: 978-1-78904-515-4 ebook: 978-1-78904-516-1

Life Before the Internet
What we can learn from the good old days
Michael Gentle
EA fascinating look back at a slower, simpler time,
when Amazon was just a river.
Paperback: 978-1-80341-388-4 ebook: 978-1-80341-389-1

Breath for Health
A Mindful Way to Restore Your Natural Breathing Cycle
Michael D Hutchinson
Discover the secrets hidden in yoga and modern physiology —
and restore your natural, healthy, confident way of
breathing in just 10 minutes a day.
Paperback: 978-1-80341-440-9 ebook: 978-1-80341-441-6

Readers of ebooks can buy or view any of these bestsellers by
clicking on the live link in the title. Most titles are published
in paperback and as an ebook. Paperbacks are available in
traditional bookshops. Both print and ebook formats are
available online.

Find more titles and sign up to our readers' newsletter at
www.o-books.com

Follow O-Books on Facebook at **O-Books**

For video content, author interviews and more, please subscribe to our YouTube channel:

O-BOOKS Presents

Follow us on social media for book news, promotions and more:

Facebook: O-Books

Instagram: @o_books_mbs

'X' (formerly Twitter): @obooks

Tik Tok: @ObooksMBS

www.o-books.com